A LOOK AT WORLD HISTORY

THE NORMAN CONQUEST

BY MARIE ROESSER

Gareth Stevens
PUBLISHING

CRASHCOURSE

Please visit our website, www.garethstevens.com. For a free color catalog of all our high-quality books, call toll free 1-800-542-2595 or fax 1-877-542-2596.

Library of Congress Cataloging-in-Publication Data

Names: Roesser, Marie, author.
Title: The Norman Conquest / Marie Roesser.
Description: New York : Gareth Stevens Publishing, [2020] | Series: A look at world history | Includes index.
Identifiers: LCCN 2018042109| ISBN 9781538241424 (pbk.) | ISBN 9781538241448 (library bound) | ISBN 9781538241431 (6 pack)
Subjects: LCSH: Great Britain--History--Norman period, 1066-1154--Juvenile literature. | William I, King of England, 1027 or 1028-1087--Juvenile literature. | Normans--Great Britain--Juvenile literature.
Classification: LCC DA195 .R83 2020 | DDC 942.02--dc23
LC record available at https://lccn.loc.gov/2018042109

First Edition

Published in 2020 by
Gareth Stevens Publishing
111 East 14th Street, Suite 349
New York, NY 10003

Designer: Katelyn E. Reynolds
Editor: Therese Shea

Photo credits: Cover, pp. 1, 17 The Print Collector/Print Collector/Getty Images; cover, pp. 1–32 (background) javarman/Shutterstock.com; cover, pp. 1–32 (border) Anastasiia Smiian/Shutterstock.com; pp. 5, 7 (inset), 11 duncan1890/DigitalVision Vectors/Getty Images; pp. 7 (map), 15 Alfonso de Tomas/Shutterstock.com; p. 9 image on website of Ulrich Harsh./Thincat/Wikipedia.org; p. 13 Illustratedjc/Wikipedia.org; p. 19 Myrabella/ Wikipedia.org; p. 21 Grzegorz_Pakula/Shutterstock.com; p. 23 Photo 12/UIG via Getty Images; p. 25 Sue Martin/Shutterstock.com; p. 27 Jonathan Brady/PA Images via Getty Images; p. 29 Supercarwaar/Tristan Surtel/Wikipedia.org.

Printed in the United States of America

CPSIA compliance information: Batch #CS19GS: For further information contact Gareth Stevens, New York, New York at 1-800-542-2595.

CONTENTS

Words in the glossary appear in **bold** type the first time they are used in the text.

DEATH OF A KING

On January 5, 1066, the king of England, Edward the Confessor, died. He had no children to become ruler after him. His decision about who would wear the crown had a lasting effect on English history. A **conquest** of England followed.

MAKE THE GRADE

In King Edward's time, a confessor was someone who lived a holy life. Edward was later named a saint by the Catholic Church.

WILLIAM VS. HAROLD

Historians believe Edward the Confessor had promised his cousin William, the duke of Normandy, that he would be king after Edward's death. William was the most powerful lord in France at that time. He wanted to be king of England, too.

WILLIAM, DUKE OF NORMANDY

MAKE THE GRADE

William became a duke when he was about 7 years old. His life was always in danger because others wanted to rule Normandy, which is in northern France.

Before Edward died, he promised the crown to a lord named Harold Godwinson. Earlier, Harold had sworn to support William as king. Some say William may have tricked him for this support. However, Harold accepted the crown and became King Harold II. William prepared to **invade** England to fight Harold.

MAKE THE GRADE

The Bayeux Tapestry is a long cloth decorated with more than 70 pictures of what would be called the Norman Conquest. This part shows Harold visiting Edward before his death.

William had the support of other Norman leaders as well as the Catholic **pope**. By August 1066, he had put together an army of more than 4,000 soldiers. However, they couldn't sail to England until the winds changed direction.

MAKE THE GRADE

The winds didn't blow in the right direction to sail to England for another 8 weeks!

MORE THREATS

Harold's brother Tostig also wanted to be king. He and King Harald III Sigurdsson of Norway joined forces and invaded the north of England. On September 25, 1066, Harold's army surprised and **defeated** them at Stamford Bridge. Tostig and Harald III were killed.

MAKE THE GRADE

King Harald III is sometimes called "Hardraade," which means "hard ruler."

WILLIAM ARRIVES

On September 27, 1066, William and his Norman army crossed the English Channel. They landed in the town of Pevensey the next day and traveled east to Hastings. On October 1, Harold and his army began to march south to meet William.

MAKE THE GRADE

Harold had placed soldiers in the south to guard against invaders in May 1066. However, they had returned home in September to pick their crops.

THE BATTLE OF HASTINGS

The English army reached Hastings on October 13. The Normans surprised them early the next morning. Harold's soldiers held their ground during the attack. A **rumor** spread that William had been killed. Hearing this, some Norman soldiers ran away.

MAKE THE GRADE

The Battle of Hastings was actually fought a few miles from Hastings, near a town called Battle.

To show that he was still alive, William took off his helmet. His soldiers returned to fighting the English. Harold was killed in battle. The Bayeaux Tapestry suggests he was shot in the eye with an arrow. Harold's soldiers ran away.

THE DEATH OF HAROLD II

MAKE THE GRADE

Harold II was the last Anglo-Saxon king of England.

KING WILLIAM

William marched on to London. The English nobles accepted his rule. He was crowned king of England at Westminster Abbey on December 25, 1066. However, he'd face **rebellions** against his rule for the next 5 years.

MAKE THE GRADE

At William's crowning, guards outside the church mistakenly thought he was being attacked inside. They set fire to nearby buildings.

One rebellion in a northern area of England called Northumbria took place from 1069 to 1070. William ordered that villages, crops, and livestock be destroyed. This punishment caused many people to go hungry and even die.

THE HARRYING OF THE NORTH

MAKE THE GRADE

Some reported that 100,000 people died after William ordered villages and farms to be burned in the north. This is called the Harrying of the North.

AFTER THE CONQUEST

The Norman Conquest changed England. William made his knights lords and gave them English land. The Normans became the most powerful people in England. They built hundreds of castles. There were more than 500 castles in England and Wales by 1087.

MAKE THE GRADE

William even replaced the heads of monasteries with Norman monks. He ordered that the monastery called Battle Abbey be built where the Battle of Hastings was fought.

After the conquest, French and Latin became the languages that people in power used in England, not English. In fact, English wasn't used again as a written language until the 1200s. Many French words became part of the English language.

MAKE THE GRADE

King William ordered that a record be kept about English lands and property so that he could tax them. The record, which still exists, is called the Domesday Book.

THE CONQUEROR DIES

In 1087, William was **injured** while fighting in France. He died on September 9 and was buried in Caen, France. His sons ruled after him. After his death, King William, the man who had changed England forever, became known as William the Conqueror.

MAKE THE GRADE

It's said that William's body didn't fit into his coffin!

KEY DATES OF THE NORMAN CONQUEST

JANUARY 5, 1066
King Edward the Confessor of England dies.

JANUARY 6, 1066
Harold Godwinson is crowned king of England.

AUGUST 1066
William of Normandy readies an invasion force.

SEPTEMBER 25, 1066
King Harold's army defeats Tostig and Harald III's forces at Stamford Bridge.

SEPTEMBER 27, 1066
William and his army cross the English Channel.

SEPTEMBER 28, 1066
William's forces land near Pevensey and travel east.

OCTOBER 1, 1066
King Harold's army marches south.

OCTOBER 13, 1066
King Harold's army reaches Hastings.

OCTOBER 14, 1066
William's army defeats Harold's forces at the Battle of Hastings.

DECEMBER 25, 1066
William is crowned king of England at Westminster Abbey.

GLOSSARY

Anglo-Saxon: a member of the Germanic people of northern central Europe who conquered Britain in the 5th century

coffin: a box in which a dead person is buried

conquest: the act of taking control of a country through the use of force

defeat: to beat

injured: harmed

invade: to enter a place to take it over

monastery: a place where religious men called monks live and work together, separated from the rest of society

pope: the head of the Roman Catholic Church

rebellion: a fight to overthrow a government

rumor: a story that is passed from person to person but has not been proven to be true

FOR MORE INFORMATION

BOOKS

Hamilton, John. *Battle of Hastings*. Minneapolis, MN: ABDO Publishing Company, 2014.

Ross, Stewart. *William the Conqueror: Guilty or Innocent?* London, England: ReadZone Books, 2017.

WEBSITES

Middle Ages: William the Conqueror
www.ducksters.com/history/middle_ages/william_the_conqueror.php
Find out more about this ruler's life.

1066: The Battle of Hastings
www.theschoolrun.com/homework-help/1066-the-battle-of-hastings
Read the top 10 facts about this famous event.

Publisher's note to educators and parents: Our editors have carefully reviewed these websites to ensure that they are suitable for students. Many websites change frequently, however, and we cannot guarantee that a site's future contents will continue to meet our high standards of quality and educational value. Be advised that students should be closely supervised whenever they access the internet.

INDEX